NAMITA BADDULA

Unboxable

Your Exit Interview from Everyone's expectations

Dear folks,
Thank you for loving me through every twist, turn, and wild idea.
To my Dad, for your unwavering faith in me.
To my Mum, for your constant care and love.
To my husband Santosh, for seeing all of me and staying anyway :)
To my brother Naren, for being my anchor when things got messy.
and my Ammama, for being my first safe space and softest love.
This book carries all of you in every word.
This book exists because you held me up even when none of it made
sense.
Love,
Namita <3

Contents

Preface

For anyone who's ever felt like too much or not enough at all
This book isn't a blueprint.
It's a rebellion.
A reclamation.
A mirror.
Unboxable is for the ones who've been told to "just pick one."
The ones who dimmed their light to be more "digestible."
The ones who've rewritten their bios 37 times, trying to sound more consistent — less confusing.
It's for the wildly creative analyst who also does energy work.
The product manager who dreams of publishing poetry.
The strategist who teaches breathwork on weekends.
The leader who's tired of being seen as *just* one thing.
It's for YOU, the person reading this. Whose life doesn't fit into a single title, neat category, or aesthetic Instagram grid.
I wrote this book because I lived this book.
I tried niching down. I tried building a "cohesive" brand. I tried becoming what the world told me was "clear."

And in the process, I lost parts of myself that I loved, the parts that made me whole.
This isn't a book about balance.
It's a book about integration.
It's about building a life, career, and identity that can hold *all* of

you, without an apology.

Inside these pages, you'll find stories, provocations, truths you've whispered to yourself in the dark, and permission slips you didn't know you were waiting for.

You'll also find reflection prompts, rituals, and frameworks not to box you in, but to help you build your own blueprint for a life that makes sense to *you*.

So if you've ever felt too multi-passionate, too loud, too emotional, too curious, too unconventional, too *anything* :

Welcome.

You're not too much.

You're *unboxable*.

And it's time the world saw you that way, too.

Chapter 1

Outgrowing the Box They Gave You

Most of us have been taught sometimes gently, sometimes forcefully, to *get in the box.*

The box is comfortable.

The box is certain.

The box is that neat little title you say at parties: "I'm a lawyer." "I work in finance." "I'm a project manager."

Inside the box, everything makes sense to everyone else.

However, over time, it starts to make less sense to you.

You feel cramped. Flattened. Over-defined.

You begin to ask questions like: *Is this it? Is this all I'm allowed to be?*

And that's when it begins: the urge to **unbox** yourself.

To stretch. To re-introduce yourself, not as one thing, but as someone *becoming many things.*

This book is a permission slip to leave the box behind, not in a reckless, *"I-don't-care-what-anyone-thinks"* kind of way, but in a conscious, spacious, soul-aligned sort of way.

Because the truth is:

The people who change the world or even just change their own lives, don't think outside the box.

They *live* outside of it.

You're at a gathering, maybe a friend's birthday or a casual work mixer. Someone new walks up and asks:

"So, what do you do?"

Your mind doesn't go blank. It floods.

You think of your job. The project you're building on the side. That course you just signed up for. The idea you've been obsessing over but haven't told anyone about.

You stall and say something safe like,

"I work in tech," or "I'm a designer," or "I'm into business."

The person nods. You smile.

But inside? A small part of you winces.

Because you didn't lie, but you definitely *shrank* the truth.

But what is the cost of being "Understandable"

You didn't mention the creative art workshop you're leading.

Or the homegrown skincare brand you're testing out.

Or your long-term dream of building a mentorship collective for women in spirituality.

Because you've learnt that the world isn't built for multidimensional people, it prefers a clean story. One that can fit in a headline, a LinkedIn bio, or a dinner party reply.

So, slowly, you've edited. Simplified. Strategically left things out.

And each time, something inside you whispers: *this isn't the whole of me.*

And when "Pick One Thing" stops working for you

Most of us didn't start out trying to be a niche.
As kids, we were encouraged to try everything. Be curious.
Explore.
But somewhere between adolescence and growing up, the message changed.
Pick a major. Pick a lane. Stick to it.
Anything less is flaky. Anything more is "too much."
You were taught that focus = success.
But what if your version of focus doesn't look like one thing for 40 years?
What if it looks like it is evolving? Expanding? Reinventing?
Trust me, that's not confusion. That's *capacity*.

What Mr. Steve Jobs Got Right

Before Steve Jobs became the icon behind Apple, he dropped out of college and took a calligraphy class.
Everyone said it was pointless.
However, years later, when he led the design of the first Macintosh, it was that class that influenced Apple's typography, layout, and signature aesthetic.
That one "useless" curiosity became one of Apple's greatest product differentiation.
Jobs didn't follow a straight line. He followed what fascinated him, and wove it into the future.

That's what multi-passionate people do.

The thing is ... You're Not Confused, You're Wired Differently

You're not messy. You're just not built to live inside one definition.

You're layered. Expansive. Maybe even a little nonlinear and that's not a problem. That's *design*.

You're like Maya Angelou, who was a fry cook, a dancer, a singer, a journalist, an activist, and a poet. Her story was not a ladder, it was a spiral staircase. And every turn gave her voice more depth.

She didn't build a brand. She built a body of work.

So why do we think our lives need to be easy to explain to be legitimate?

Let us look at The Lady Gaga Principle

And then there's Lady Gaga.

Musician. Actress. Activist. Fashion disruptor. Mental health advocate. Cultural shapeshifter.

She's won the Grammy's and the Oscars, launched foundations, and played sold-out stadiums, *without* ever picking one lane.

One moment she's in a meat dress, the next she's delivering a tearful speech about trauma recovery or starring in a critically acclaimed drama.

She didn't apologize for her range. She made the world stretch to meet it.

That's what makes her magnetic.

She's not confused. She's *uncontainable*.

And so are you.

Now you don't have to be Lady Gaga or Jobs to Justify Your Layers

Here's the good news: you don't need to be a global icon to live like you're unboxed.

You just need to stop asking, "Which one of these things is the real me?"

And start asking, "What kind of life can hold *all* of me?"

You don't need to fit into a format.

You need to create your own.

Let us talk about The Quiet Burnout No One Talks About

There's a special kind of burnout that happens when you keep compartmentalizing your joy.

You go to work and leave your creative self at the door.

You build a business but silence your inner healer.

You brand yourself as one thing and quietly grieve all the parts that didn't make the cut.

It's not that you're doing too much.

It's that you're doing too little of what feels *whole*.

Approaching A Different Kind of 'Structure'

Let's be real: you can't do *everything* at once.
But you don't need to. Being multi-passionate doesn't mean chaos, it means building your own rhythm.
This book isn't here to help you niche down. It's here to help you design a life where your interests *coexist*, not compete.
This is about building a system that *fits you*, not forcing yourself to fit a system.
Or not!
You do YOU. Ultimately we want to live Unboxed.

Let's Start With This

Let's get one thing straight: this book won't change your life if you just read it like a blog post and keep scrolling.
You don't *consume* this book. You live it.
You answer it. You wrestle with it. You call yourself out in the margins.
If you're just nodding along and underlining quotes to post on Instagram later, you're missing the whole damn point.
This isn't a vibe.
It's a reckoning.
And I say that with love.
Because here's the deal:
You've spent enough years smoothing your edges, shrinking your story, and editing your weirdness to fit the brand. You've

already mastered being marketable.

What you haven't been taught is how to be *whole.*

So when a question comes up in these pages, don't skim past it like it's extra credit.

Answer it like your freedom depends on it.

Because maybe it does.

You can't unbox your life without getting your hands messy.

And if you're here to stay safe, sound smart, and protect your polished version of self — this book will disappoint you.

But if you're here to be *real.* As in full, messy, magic-in-progress you?

Then baby, welcome home.

Now let's *actually* begin.

Ask yourself:

"What part of me have I been hiding just to seem easier to understand?"

That answer?

That's the part we're bringing back online.

Because your clarity doesn't come from being one thing.

It comes from learning how to move through the world as *all* of you.

The people who are hardest to define are often the ones changing the game. Not because they chose a lane, but because they created one.

That's what you're here to do.

And we're just getting started.

Chapter 2

The Multi-Passionate Manifesto

There's a moment, often sometime after you've tried to follow the "one thing" rule, when you realize... it's just not working.
You've tried to focus.
Tried to pick one lane.
Tried to silence the part of you that lights up when something *else* sparks your interest.
But the restlessness doesn't go away.
Not because you're flaky.
But because you're *wired for more.*
Let's get one thing straight before we go any further:
You're not all over the place. You're not flaky.
You're not broken. You're just *built differently.*
And the world hasn't quite caught up to people like you.

The Labels You've Outgrown

People like to call us "scattered."
That's the polite version. The kinder cousin of "unfocused,"
"all over the place," or "lacking direction."
But here's the truth: most people don't actually know how to
handle multi-dimensionality. So they label it.
Think of labels like:

- "Jack of all trades, master of none"
- "Serial hobbyist"
- "Always chasing the next shiny thing"

But the real story underneath?
You're a connector. A synthesizer. A creative. A system thinker.
A lifelong learner.
What looks like chaos to others is often a *pattern they haven't
learned to read yet.*

Asha's Story: The Pattern in the Pivot

Let's take Asha.She started her career in architecture. Three
years in, she moved to UX design. Then pivoted into service
design. Later, she took a sabbatical and studied Ayurvedic
healing and now she combines design thinking and wellness
in corporate workshops. People in her life used to ask, "Are
you sure this is the right path?" And Asha would smile because
she finally saw what they didn't: Her work was never about
buildings, or apps, or healing protocols. It was about how

people interact with space, systems, and themselves.She wasn't scattered. She was zoomed out.

That's what being multi-passionate looks like.

It's not chaos. It's a constellation.

What's Really Going On in a Multi-Passionate Brain

When you're wired like this, you tend to:

- Pick things up quickly.
- Get bored easily.
- See connections where others don't.
- Shift identities across seasons.
- Obsess over learning, then move on when mastery hits.

It can feel like a curse if you don't know what's happening.

But it's not a bug, it's a feature.

People like you are often *systems disruptors*, *creative catalysts*, and *unofficial futurists*.

You don't just operate within categories.

You *redefine them*.

What If You Reframed "Scattered" as "Layered"?

Let's flip some scripts:

When you stop internalizing judgment, you can start designing a life that matches how you *really* function.

Not everyone will understand your path.

They don't need to.
What matters is that *you* do.

When You Don't Fit the Script

What They Say		What's Actually True
"You lack focus."	⟶	"You have layered attention."
"You keep changing direction."	⟶	"You adapt quickly and follow alignment."
"You're indecisive."	⟶	"You're curious and wide-visioned."
"You don't know what you want."	⟶	"You've outgrown what no longer fits."

There is a script most of us were handed early on in our lives, and it goes like :

- Find your one true calling
- Build a career around it
- Stay consistent
- Keep leveling up in that lane

And if you deviate? You'll look like a dilettante.
Or with, you won't be taken seriously.
So when you're someone with layered interests, who thrives on variety, who can shift gears faster than most people change their coffee order, you start to feel like the outlier.

You ask yourself, *"What's wrong with me?"*
But the better question is: *"What if there's nothing wrong at all?"*

My Story: Tech by Day, Healer by Heart

Let me bring you into my world for a moment.
I've spent most of my professional life in tech. I led teams. I handled stakeholder calls with global clients. I discussed KPI's, Jira boards, and product lifecycles. I wrote documentation. I trained analysts. I was and I still am deeply embedded in the logical, structured, measurable world of IT.
But at the same time?
I was learning how to channel energy.
I became a certified Reiki healer. I began studying the Akashic Records, learning how to access spiritual blueprints, soul histories, and inner truths that aren't found on spreadsheets or sprint boards.
There were nights when I'd go from running a release planning meeting to conducting a distance healing session for a woman navigating grief, or reading the Akashic Records for someone in Australia who felt lost in her career but hadn't yet named it.
I didn't talk about this side much at first.
Because, well... how do you tell your tech colleagues you're moonlighting as an intuitive channel?
But here's what I realized:
I wasn't living two lives. I was living a rich, multi-dimensional one.
The skills I developed in tech made me a better healer, structured, precise, grounded and the spiritual path gave me the capacity to lead, hold space, and *listen* in ways that transformed how I showed up at work.

They didn't cancel each other out.
They *complemented* each other.

The Language of Layers

When you're multi-passionate, your identity doesn't fit into one container. It spills into several.
It's tempting to try to streamline your story to make it palatable for recruiters, family members, clients, or even your own inner critic. But every time you do, you're likely leaving something vital out.
Your story isn't broken. It's *layered*.
And that's a different kind of brilliance.

The Problem Isn't Curiosity - It's Expectation

If you've ever felt shame for wanting to do "too many things," ask yourself, where did that shame come from?
Probably from people who feel safer when others are easier to define.
But curiosity is not chaos.
Curiosity is a sign of aliveness.
You're allowed to want to learn, build, explore, pause, quit, start over, do more than one thing, and still be seen as intelligent, credible, and professional.
You're allowed to evolve without having to justify every step.
You're allowed to be the kind of person who lives in seasons, not job titles.

What "Scattered" Actually Looks Like

When someone calls you scattered, what they might really mean is:

- "You're hard to categorize."
- "You don't fit my mental checklist."
- "You're growing in ways I don't understand."

But what's actually happening inside you?

- You're deeply observant.
- You see patterns before they emerge.
- You feel your way through life instead of forcing your way through it.
- You don't settle into one identity, because you keep expanding.

Famous, Multi-Passionate, and Unapologetic

Let's bring in **Emma Watson**.
Most people know her as Hermione Granger from the Harry Potter series. But Emma didn't stop at acting.
She graduated from Brown University.
She became a UN Women Goodwill Ambassador.
She launched a sustainable fashion initiative.
She actively supports causes around climate justice, education, and gender equality.
She could have played it safe. She stuck to one thing and coasted

off her fame.

But she didn't.

She followed what mattered, even when it meant evolving past what the world expected of her.

Emma is not scattered. She's sovereign.

She doesn't ask for permission to shift. She just does it with care, with clarity, with purpose.

How to Start Seeing Your Own Pattern

Here's what I want you to ask yourself:

"If I looked at my life like a constellation instead of a career ladder, what connects my dots?"

Maybe it's the way you always create space for people to be heard.

Or your obsession with systems, whether they're business models or astrology charts.

Maybe it's your instinct to teach, even when no one gave you the title.

Or your ability to take raw ideas and translate them into real, working frameworks — whether in a codebase, a coaching session, or a kitchen.

When you zoom out, you'll start to see:

Your path isn't messy. It's *multi-dimensional.*

You Don't Need to Choose. You Need to Integrate.

Being multi-passionate doesn't mean you do everything at once.
It means you allow for more than one version of yourself to exist,
over time, and sometimes even at the same time.
You don't need to split yourself to be taken seriously.
You don't need to shut down parts of your personality to get
hired, followed, or funded.
You don't need to label your joy as a "distraction" just because
it doesn't fit the mould.
You just need a framework that makes space for *you*, not the
idea of you.

Your Energy Is Not "Too Much"

Your energy is wide. Expansive. Bold.
It may not move in straight lines.
It may not sound like a perfect elevator pitch.
But it holds magic, wisdom, and momentum when you stop
trying to flatten it into a job title.
You're not here to be easy to explain.
You're here to be fully expressed.

You're Not Lost , You're Listening

If you're in a season where you feel unsure, in-between, or "unfinished," that doesn't mean you've failed.
It means you're listening.
Listening to what calls you next. Listening to what no longer fits. Listening to your deeper design.
And when you build your life in that kind of alignment, the need to pick one thing becomes irrelevant.
Because you're no longer choosing between clarity and creativity.
You're creating a *new kind of clarity*, one that belongs to you.

Let's Redefine What Success Looks Like

Imagine this:
A life that holds your range without guilt.
A career that flexes with your interests.
A rhythm that honors your seasons.
A story that includes your pivots, your pauses, your passions — without apology.
That's what you're building.
That's what being *Unboxable* is about.
You're not scattered.
You're just unshakably *you*, and you're done hiding it.

Chapter 3

The Curse of Being "On Brand"

There's a moment that hits you in the middle of building your so-called "personal brand."
You've refined your elevator pitch.
You've curated your posts.
You've adjusted your story to make sense to others.
You've simplified the chaos into something clean and clickable.
And then one day, you wake up and wonder,
"Is this even me anymore?"

The Invisible Line Between Strategy and Self-Abandonment

We're taught that clarity is the holy grail. That if people "get" you fast, you win. If they can put you in a box, you'll be rewarded. If they can categorise you, they'll trust you.
So we start the pruning.
We keep the parts of our story that sound sharp, digestible, and impressive.We trim the parts that feel "too much," "too weird," "too hard to explain."
And slowly, we disappear; one polished line at a time.

My Story: The "Tech Expert" Who Left Pieces Behind

There was a time in my career when the only version of me that existed publicly was the "tech leader."
The engineering manager. The business analyst mentor. The product thinker.
I was giving talks, building programs, and mentoring business analysts across the world. On paper, I looked laser-focused. Refined. Clear.
But in real life?
I was learning Reiki.
I was reading soul contracts in Akashic Records.
I was painting, crafting, and sculpting.
I was healing and helping others heal.
And not a single trace of that showed up in my "brand."
Because somewhere along the way, I believed I had to pick.
Be technical or be mystical.

Be strategic or be soft.
Be successful or be soulful.
And I couldn't find anyone around me who held *both* visibly, unapologetically.
So I split.
Not in a dramatic way. In a slow, quiet, "maybe I'll just leave that out" kind of way.
And the more I leaned into the version of myself that got applauded as the technical expert, the more I felt like I was losing air.

When Curated Clarity become a Cage

It wasn't that I hated what I was doing. I *loved* mentoring analysts. I *thrived* in strategic conversations. But I couldn't shake the feeling that I was performing a version of myself, instead of *being* myself.
People would say things like,
"You're such a powerhouse of tech clarity."
And I'd smile. And thank them. And then quietly wonder why it made me feel hollow.
Because what they were seeing, while true, wasn't the full picture.
And what's the point of being seen... if you're not actually being seen?

The Alicia Keys Shift

Now, let me share a story that helped me give myself permission to let go of the polish.
A few years ago, Alicia Keys, a 5-time Grammy-winning artist, made a very public decision:
She stopped wearing makeup.
To some, it sounded trivial. But for her, it was seismic.
She had spent years as a brand, an image, a voice, a persona.
She was always "on." Always performing. Always polished.
Until she realized she was no longer sure where the persona ended and she began.
So she walked away from it.
She showed up bare-faced. Stripped back. Real.
And the world didn't fall apart.
She was no less powerful.
If anything, she was *more* magnetic.
Because she no longer needed to perform clarity.
She was choosing *authenticity*.

What Clarity Actually Means (And Doesn't)

Clarity has become a buzzword, especially in personal development and career coaching spaces.

- "Get clear on your niche."
- "Have a crystal-clear message."
- "Clarity converts."

But no one warns you what happens when clarity turns into constraint.

Clarity is supposed to mean: *you know who you are.*

But it's often misused to mean: *you've made yourself easy to explain to others.*

Those are not the same thing.

The Danger of Branding Too Early

Sometimes, people brand themselves before they've even figured out who they are.

You pick a lane too soon. You commit to a version of you that made sense at the time. But then you evolve... and the brand doesn't.

Now you're stuck in a container you outgrew.

Like the career coach who no longer wants to coach careers.

Or the mindset influencer who's secretly burned out on motivation.

Or the tech mentor who also wants to talk about soul alchemy but doesn't know how to blend the two without losing her audience.

So you keep the brand. And lose yourself.

That's not clarity. That's captivity.

The Inner Conflict of Consistency

There's also this weird pressure to be *consistent* online.
Post the same thing. Speak in the same tone. Be "on brand."
But real humans aren't consistent. They're cyclical. Emotional.
Expansive. Complex.
Your voice might change.
Your focus might shift.
Your truth might evolve.
And when you build a brand based only on *what's easy to market*,
you risk amputating the parts of you that are still unfolding.
Eventually, you'll reach a point where you either:

- Keep the performance going, and feel dead inside
- Or risk being misunderstood, and feel *free*

Guess which one this book is rooting for?

What I Did Next

When I finally let go of the need to be *just* the tech mentor,
something cracked open.
I began showing my art again. I started talking, softly at first,
about my healing work. I wove in mysticism, creativity, and soul
work alongside stakeholder management and Agile workflows.
I didn't create "two brands."
I just let myself be one whole person, "publicly."
And guess what?
People didn't run.

They leaned in.

Because they were *also* hiding layers.

And I going first, permitted them to bring theirs back online.

That's the thing about authenticity, it doesn't repel people. It reminds them of themselves.

Granted, you will still have outliers, but hey, it's progress and a happier and more truthful one at that.

From Personal Brand to Personal Truth

You don't need a personal brand.

You need personal *alignment*.

A personal brand is often about perception. Personal alignment is about *wholeness*.

And when you lead with alignment, you'll still attract opportunities — but they'll be the *right* ones. The ones that match who you *actually* are.

Let's be real: there's no amount of visibility worth losing your voice over.

If You Feel Like You're Hiding

Let's call it out.

If you've been:

- Avoiding posting because you don't want to sound fake
- Hiding certain parts of your life because they don't "fit"

your narrative
- Feeling flat about your own content or your career
- Confused about why your work doesn't feel like *you* anymore

It might not be burnout.
It might be branding fatigue.
You don't need to rebrand.
You need to *reclaim.*

What to Do Instead

So what do you do when you want to show up honestly, but your brand is built around one version of you?
Here's what helped me:

1. Stop seeing clarity as a final destination.

Clarity is seasonal. What's true for you now may evolve, and that's okay.

You launched a program last year about productivity, but now you're more drawn to teaching energy work. That shift isn't failure, it's clarity and it is evolving in real time.

2. Allow your content to reflect your growth.

Even if it means changing direction. Even if people don't "get it" right away.
One month you're posting about career pivots, the next you're

talking about your journey into healing. That's not inconsis-tency, that's your real time experience and you being honest.

3. Anchor into values, not labels.

Instead of identifying as "the strategist" or "the healer," ask: What do I stand for? What do I care about? What do I bring to every room, regardless of role?
Whether you're on a tech panel or guiding a breathwork circle, you always bring curiosity, depth, and empowerment. That's your *core*, not the title you're introduced with.

4. Blend, don't compartmentalize.

If you're spiritual and strategic, show it. If you're tech-savvy and intuitive, own it. Let your range *become* your voice.
Stop treating your skills like they belong in separate drawers. You don't have to be strategic *or* spiritual, you can be BOTH in the same conversation, the same offer, and the same day.

The World Is Craving Wholeness

We are tired of polished performances.
We want nuance. We want contradiction. We want truth.
People don't connect to perfect brands.
They connect to real stories. Full stories. Imperfect, honest, evolving stories.
And that means showing up in your *humanity*, not just your strategy.

You can be clear and still be curious.
You can be focused and still fluid.
You can be magnetic without being manicured.
Clarity isn't the absence of complexity.
It's the presence of self-trust.

You're Allowed to Change

One of the bravest things you can do is say:
"This version of me is no longer true. And I'm ready to show you the new one."
Not everyone will understand the shift.
But the people who matter will feel it.
And they'll find you in the *realness*, not the polish.
If you've been feeling like you're losing yourself inside your brand, let this chapter be your permission slip.
To change.
To return.
To expand.
To tell the truth.
Because clarity without authenticity is just performance.
But when you reclaim your full voice even the messy, magical, multidimensional parts — that's when you become unforgettable.
Not for the way you package yourself.
But for the way you *finally let yourself be seen.*

Chapter 4

Tired of Performing? Good. That Means You're Waking Up.

Let's start with a truth most of us are too polite to say out loud: **Pretending to be simple is exhausting.**

Not simple as in minimal or peaceful — we're all for that.

But simple as in *predictable*. One-track. Easy to explain. Boxed up, wrapped tight, branded neatly.

You become the one who "has it all figured out." The one who fits the bio. The one who knows her niche.

And at some point, you even start believing the script.

Until one day, you don't.

You can't.

Because the version of you that you've been performing has stopped feeling like you.

The Hidden Exhaustion of Playing Small

Let me tell you something that still makes me flinch when I think about it:
There was a time in my life; not that long ago, when I would laugh *along* with my friends as they joked about "all that woo-woo stuff."
Crystals. Energy work. Spirit guides. Akashic Records.
Eventually, something inside me started breaking.
Not loudly. Not dramatically. But quietly, in moments that no one else saw.
Like when I'd laugh along with a joke about "that woo stuff" — while a part of me winced on the inside.Or when I'd listen to friends talk about logic and strategy and goals — and bite my tongue about the journey I'd been quietly exploring behind closed doors.
I was the techie. The team lead. The "put-together" one who knew how to speak to cranky stakeholders.
What no one knew is the alter ego I had, where I already started reading the Akashic Records.
I hadn't told anyone. Not because I wasn't sure of it, but because I wasn't sure *I* would be taken seriously. I was still a techie. The dependable one. The one who knew how to present at client meetings without flinching.
Not the one who could sit with people's karmic wounds and watch them cry through truth they'd been avoiding for years.
But I was doing that too.
Late at night.
On weekends.
In quiet sessions with people who needed something deeper than surface-level advice.

And every time I did, it felt like I was coming home to a part of myself I didn't know I had lost.

I didn't plan to "become" spiritual.

It wasn't a goal. It was more like something old waking up in me.

Reiki came later. Not as a next step. More like a missing piece I didn't know I needed.

I wasn't looking to add another skill. I was trying to stay grounded, because sometimes what I saw in the Records felt like too much to hold alone.

And still... I kept it quiet.

I'd log into work calls and switch that part of me off like a light.

I told myself it was easier that way.

But it wasn't.

It felt like hiding. Like betraying something sacred just to be easier to understand.

And that kind of hiding wears you down in ways you don't even realize — until one day, you do.

Things that were *my truth*.

Things that *lit me up*.

I kept those other parts quiet. Tucked away.

I let the jokes pass. I smiled through them. I played it cool.

And later, alone, I'd feel it, that bitter after pill.

It wasn't rage. It wasn't shame.

It was something worse: *grief*.

Grief for the version of me I abandoned to be easier for other people to understand.

The Invisible Weight of Being Palatable

Being palatable doesn't sound like a big deal. But if you've lived it, you know.
You keep the "safe" parts on display, the job title, the industry credibility, the easily explained wins.
You hide the parts that spark you, the art, the intuition, the softness, the side passions, the sacred mess.
And you slowly start to feel like a half-version of yourself.
You're visible, sure. But it's like being seen in low resolution.
You walk into rooms where everyone claps for the version of you that performs best, and silently mourn the version of you that never got to speak.

The Sushmita Sen Blueprint

And then there's Sushmita Sen.
Miss Universe at 18. National darling. Beauty queen. Actress.
Every headline tried to shape her into something digestible: glamorous, elegant, poised.
But she never stayed where people placed her.
She became a single mother at a time when it was unheard of — adopting her first daughter at 24. She didn't ask for validation. She just *did it.*
She refused to marry for optics. She built her career rhythm.
She spoke with the calm defiance of a woman who never needed to be made simpler to be taken seriously.
Sushmita never performed palatability.
She chose truth over approval.

Layers over clarity.
Sovereignty over branding.
She is *living proof* that being fully yourself, even when it confuses people — is the most radical clarity there is.

What Performing Simplicity Looks Like

It's not always loud. It's not always fake smiles and big lies. Sometimes, it's subtle.

- You stay silent when a topic close to your heart comes up because it's "off-brand."
- You shrink your introduction at events because your full story takes too long to explain.
- You nod along in conversations that make you feel like a tourist in your own life.
- You leave out the poem, the dream, the other degree, the healing work, the art, the "weird" idea, not because you're ashamed, but because you're *tired*.

Tired of explaining.
Tired of defending.
Tired of being a FAQ page about yourself.

The Burnout No One Warns You About

Most people talk about burnout like it's a product of *doing too much.*
But there's another kind.
The burnout that comes from pretending to be simple.
When you spend months or years performing one flattened version of yourself, it chips away at your joy. You forget what lights you up. You stop listening to your instincts.
You become someone who's always "on," but rarely *in it.*
That's what pretending does.
It drains the colour from your voice.
It turns your life into a highlight reel that feels like a stranger's.

Why You Started Performing in the First Place

This part matters.
You didn't fake it because you're weak.
You edited yourself because it felt *safer.*
At some point, you learned that being your full, layered self made people uncomfortable.
Maybe you were told you were "too intense," "too dreamy," "too sensitive," "too serious," "too scattered," or "too ambitious."
So you began the great flattening.
You tucked yourself into a more acceptable shape.
But here's the thing about palatable identities:
They're only sustainable if you stay hungry.
And one day, your hunger for authenticity gets louder than your

need to be liked.

What Freedom Begins to Feel Like

Freedom doesn't start with a big announcement.
It starts with tiny rebellions.
You say, "Actually, I do energy work," the next time someone mocks it.
You post the thing that feels true, even if it doesn't "fit your niche."
You let yourself show up messy, layered, alive, and let the world adjust.
You stop explaining.
Stop diluting.
Stop making yourself digestible to people who will never be the ones you're here to serve anyway.

What if You Let Them See All of It?

Here's the invitation:
What if you stopped curating the simplest version of yourself and started living the most *honest* one?
What if your voice cracked a little when you told your story, not because you were unsure, but because you were *feeling* it?
What if your Instagram bio wasn't optimised for conversion but for resonance?
What if your conversations went,

"Here's what I do. Here's what I love. Here's what I *am* — and no, it doesn't all fit in one line. But it's mine."

The Permission to Be "Too Much"

Let them say you're hard to define.
Let them roll their eyes at your range.
Let them call your work "too deep," your path "too weird," your dreams "too big."
Let them not get it.
That's not your problem.
Because you didn't come here to make sense.
You came here to make something *real.*

If This Chapter Feels Personal, That's Because It Is

You're probably not reading this chapter because you love branding yourself.
You're reading it because you've *felt* the fatigue of being branded.
And I want you to hear this:
You are allowed to shift.
You are allowed to say, "That's no longer me."
You are allowed to uncurate.
You are allowed to walk away from the identity that everyone loved, but you outgrew.
You are allowed to return to yourself.

Let's Make This Tangible

Here are a few questions to ask yourself if you're ready to stop performing simplicity:

1. What's one truth I've been hiding because I think it doesn't "fit" my brand?
2. What's one topic I *wish* I could speak about more openly, but I've been avoiding?
3. Where in my life am I choosing palatability over peace?
4. What would it look like to show up as the *whole* me, even if it confused people?

What is it that you need to do?

Performing one version of yourself might get you likes, applause, or even a little stability.
But it will never give you peace.
Because peace lives where all your pieces are embraced.
Where you are wildly, and weirdly wired, for some, but you do you.
Where your brand doesn't define you, your being does.
So if you're tired of pretending to be simple?
Good.
That means your whole self is waking up.
Let her speak. Let her dance. Let her post. Let her build.
You've been clear long enough.

Now it's time to be *true*.

Chapter 5

Permission to Make No Sense (and Still Be Magnetic)

There comes a point in every multi-passionate person's journey where someone, well-meaning or not, drops the line:
"I'm sorry... I just don't get what you do."
You pause. Smile. Nod politely.
Because if you had a rupee for every time someone said that?
You'd have enough to build a temple for all your passions and fund your startup dreams.
But here's the twist:
It's not *you* they don't get.
It's the **absence of a box** that's confusing them.
And that's not your problem to solve.

When Your Life Doesn't Add Up (On Purpose)

There was a time when a friend looked at me and asked, with genuine confusion,
"So... are you a business analyst, or like... some kind of spiritual therapist? And also... you make clay stuff?"
I almost choked on my chai.
In that moment, I had two options:

- Panic and try to simplify.
- Laugh and own it.

Spoiler: I laughed.
Because I had finally reached a point where I no longer needed to explain my life like a LinkedIn headline.
Yes, I lead tech strategy.
Yes, I read the Akashic Records and do energy healing.
Yes, I sculpt altar pieces out of clay.
Yes, I run career mentorship cohorts.
And no, it doesn't make clean sense — until you *feel* the pattern.
I stopped needing to be understood.
Because I was finally busy being **myself**.

The Exhaustion of Explaining Yourself

Here's the thing: you *can* explain your whole story if you really want to. You could make a neat little timeline. Draft a mission statement. List your overlapping values.
And still, some people will say,

"I don't get it."
Or
"How do you have the time for it?"
Or worse,
"You're doing too much."
These people don't need better explanations.
They need better imaginations.
You weren't made to be a punchline or a pitch deck.You were made to *live*, and sometimes that life won't be linear, filtered, or brand-friendly.
Let it be complex.
Let it be blurry in all the right places.

Frida Didn't Fit Either

Let's talk about Frida Kahlo.
Was she a painter? A political force? A style icon? A rebel? A cultural enigma?
Yes. And.
Frida didn't paint pretty pictures, she painted her spine. Her grief. Her rage. Her contradictions. Her self.
She didn't care if people thought she was *too much*.
She didn't seek clarity.
She sought *expression*.
Her art didn't fit into neat categories. Her life didn't follow respectable timelines. And her presence was so raw, people didn't know whether to admire or fear her.
And yet, here we are. Still talking about her. Still moved by her refusal to dilute her essence.

Frida didn't need to make sense to everyone.
She just needed to be **unmistakably her**.
And so do you.

You're Not a TED Talk : You're a Tapestry

Repeat this until it rewires your nervous system:
You don't have to make sense to everyone.
You're allowed to have a career path that's more *tapestry* than *timeline*.
You're allowed to say, "I do a few things — and I love that about myself."
You're allowed to exist without every strand of your story having a bullet point or a business model.
You are not a pitch.
You are a person.
People who try to *understand* you will ask for a clean story.
People who try to *connect* with you will lean in anyway.

That One Version They Wanted

You know what makes people uncomfortable?
Wholeness.
Because the world loves a single storyline.
You're either the tech expert or the spiritual weirdo.
The artist or the strategist.
The founder or the healer.

But when you start blending those roles, integrating them, speaking from your *center* instead of your label?
Some people short-circuit.
And honestly? That's not yours to fix.
Because your job is not to flatten yourself for their peace of mind.
Your job is to hold your complexity with grace, with grit, and with a little mischief.

Real Talk: You've Probably Already Tried Explaining

Let's be honest. If you're reading this chapter, chances are you've already:

- Written five different bios trying to "sum yourself up."
- Practiced answering "So what do you do?" in under 10 seconds.
- Ever wondered if you'd be taken more seriously if you just focused on *one* thing.

And every time, you felt the same ache:
You were becoming more *clear* to others and less *true* to yourself.
Let that be your red flag.
You weren't put here to be a tidy little concept.
You were put here to *embody contradiction with conviction.*

Permission to Not Be a Niche

Here's your permission slip:
You can be multi talented without becoming a brand strategy project.
You don't need a niche.
You need *a spine,* and a life that supports it.
Your clarity doesn't come from choosing between your identities.
It comes from choosing *yourself,* even when others can't follow the plot.

What I Do Now

These days, when someone asks me what I do, I no longer default to one identity.
Sometimes I say,
"I help people build careers they actually want to wake up to."
Other days, it's,
"I work at the intersection of intuition and infrastructure."
And sometimes I just smile and say,
"It's hard to explain. But people who need it, will find me."
Because it's true.
The ones who *get* it don't need bullet points.
And the ones who don't? Weren't my people anyway.

For the Times You Feel Misunderstood

If you've ever been asked,
"So what do you actually *do*?"
And felt the sting of having your story reduced to a soundbite...
If you've ever been told,
"You'd be more successful if you just focused,"
As if your joy was an inconvenience...
If you've ever tried to edit yourself into a version that fits into a dinner party conversation, but left that room feeling like a ghost of your full self...
Let me say this with my whole heart:
You're allowed to live a life that's not a single sentence long.

Try This (Even If It Feels Slightly Petty)

Next time someone says,
"I don't really understand what you do,"
Try responding with:
"That's okay. It's not for everyone to understand."
And then carry on, powerfully, calmly, and with zero urge to over explain.
Watch what happens.
Spoiler: the world doesn't end.
But your power gets a little louder.

Words you need to stick by

You don't owe anyone a perfect narrative.
Not your family.
Not your friends.
Not your clients.
Not even your audience.
You owe yourself a life that makes you feel alive, not one that makes others feel comfortable.
You don't have to make sense to everyone.
You just have to feel at *home* with yourself.
And you do that not by simplifying your truth, but by *standing in it.*
Even if they don't get it.
Even if they never do.
Especially then.

Chapter 6

"What Do You Do?" and Other Traps for Complex
Souls

Let's start with a universal truth no one likes to admit:
Introducing yourself when you do a lot feels like walking into
a party with a glitter cannon you're not sure you're allowed to
fire.
You've got all this brilliance. All these layers.
But the moment someone asks,
"So... what do you do?"
you feel like a contestant on *Who Wants to Be Understood in 10
Seconds or Less.*
Cue the panic.
Do I say the one thing I get paid for?
Do I say the thing that sounds impressive?
Do I mention the weird but wonderful side gig?
Do I tell them about the healing work, the tech consulting, the
course I'm building, the oracle deck I'm designing, the client
I'm ghostwriting for?
...Or do I just say, "It's complicated," and sip my drink like a

mystery?
Yeah. Been there.

Why Traditional Intros Suck for Multi-passionates

Let's be real: usual intros were not built for people like us.
They were built for people with a clean linear path, a one-word identity, and a LinkedIn headline that makes hiring managers salivate.
We don't live like that.
We live in loops.
In side quests.
In passion projects and professional pivots.
In sentences that don't end with a title but with an *ellipsis*.
So stop trying to jam your nonlinear magic into a single damn noun.
You're not "just" a coach.
Not "just" a strategist.
Not "just" a healer, or a coder, or a founder, or an artist.
You're a walking multiverse.
And yes, it's *okay* if it takes more than 12 words to describe yourself. The right people will listen. The wrong ones can scroll.

Your Introduction Is Not a Confession

Let's clear something up.
Talking about what you do is not a confession.
It's not a defence.
It's not a justification.
It's a declaration.
It's you owning your own weird, wonderful, wild little cocktail of skills, passions, and purpose, without apologizing for how strong it hits.
It's not your job to simplify your truth so someone else can file it neatly into a mental folder.

Here's What I Do (Depending on the Day)

Let's break the fourth wall.
Here are some ways I introduce myself, depending on the context, mood, and audience:
1. The Short & Spicy Version (when I don't have the energy to explain):
"I build things for smart people who want soulful lives — and for soulful people who want to do smart things."
2. The Bold One (when I want to magnetize the right clients):
"I help tech professionals, especially women, unlearn boring career advice and build personal brands that actually match who they are, not who they think they're supposed to be."
3. The Wild Card (when I'm in a space that feels sacred):
"I'm a strategist who speaks corporate and cosmic. I work with everything from business models to energy fields."

4. The Funny-But-True One (for nosy uncles and auntys or networking events):

"I talk for a living. Sometimes to people. Sometimes to spreadsheets. Sometimes to spirit guides."

Each one is true.

Each one is *me*.

And none of them is *all* of me.

That's the point.

The "This & That" Identity Builder

Let's be honest, when you do a lot of different things, introducing yourself can feel like a mini identity crisis. Do you lead with your day job? Your side hustle? Your soul work? Your new favourite addiction?

This framework is here to save you from awkward silences and long-winded explanations.

The magic? Contrast.

When you pair two unexpected parts of yourself, like corporate strategy and cosmic downloads, or data analysis and inner child healing, you show people the *range* you hold without watering yourself down.

Use this tool to create intros that feel spicy, soulful, or straight-up sassy, depending on your vibe. And don't overthink it. You're not trying to impress anyone. You're just letting your truth breathe a little louder.

Ready to play?

Let's fill in some blanks and find the version of *you* that feels the most real, today.

There are two frameworks that you can use and you can choose the one the feels more YOU today.

Framework 1 :

Formula:
"I [verb] for [type of people] who want [thing A] — and for [type of people] who want [thing B]."
Example:

- I design systems for chaotic creatives who crave structure and for overthinkers who secretly want to break the rules.
- I teach business analysis to storytellers who think they aren't technical and techies who want to say more than "as per the requirement."
- I build safe spaces for leaders who feel too soft and for sensitives who are secretly leaders.

Fill in Yours:

"I [] for [] who want [] — and for [] who want [________________]."

Framework 2 :
If you like something more playful, try this intro:
"Sometimes I talk to [noun]. Sometimes I talk to [contrasting noun]."
   Examples:

- Sometimes I talk to spreadsheets. Sometimes I talk to spirit guides.

- Sometimes I build dashboards. Sometimes I pull oracle cards.
- Sometimes I coach people. Sometimes I just hold space for them to breathe.

So stop looking for the perfect Sentence.

Aim for the sentence that feels like a wink at your real self.

You don't need a tagline. You need a *tone*.
You need to sound like *you*, in the wild, unfiltered, radiant version that doesn't need to explain why her story zigzags.
The goal isn't to make everyone go, "Oh, I get it."
The goal is to make the *right* people lean in and go, "Wait... tell me more."

What You're Actually Doing (When You Say What You Do)

You're not giving your life history.
You're giving a *vibe*.
You're showing someone the way you move through the world.
Are you the kind of person who blends tech and intuition?
Who builds systems and teaches somatics?
Who makes spreadsheets sing and clay speak?
Great. Say *that*.
Let it sound like a story. Like a scene. Like a conversation they'd *actually* want to have.

Because real ones don't want titles.
They want texture.

For the Ones Who Get It

There are people out there who are waiting for someone *exactly like you* — someone who isn't afraid to be more than one thing. Someone who can:

- Write code and teach breathwork
- Run a business and make intuitive art
- Read user stories and Akashic Records
- Facilitate retrospectives and rituals
- Build funnels and make reiki-infused candles

They don't want a robot. They want *range.*
Your job is not to shrink that to sound "professional."
Your job is to learn how to say it without flinching.
And that starts with saying it to yourself.

For When You're Feeling Awkward

If you ever feel awkward about "sounding like too much," here's your script:
"I do a mix of things. I like it that way."
That's it. That's the tweet. That's the boundary.
You don't owe anyone a TED Talk.

You're allowed to be complex and chill about it.
That in itself is a whole new paradigm.

Remember This

You are not:

- Confusing
- Inconsistent
- Scattered
- Indecisive

You are:

- Evolving
- Expansive
- Expressive
- Embodied

Your introduction doesn't have to make you sound employable.
It has to make you feel *seen*.

What do you do next ?

The next time someone asks,
"What do you do?"
Try this:

Say it with your heart. Say it with your weirdness. Say it like the future version of you is already clapping from the sidelines.

And if they don't get it?

Let that be their problem.

Because you're not here to be summed up.

You're here to *take up space* — and maybe blow a few minds while you're at it.

REMEMBER....

You're not a damn LinkedIn headline.

You're a revolution in motion.

And anyone who needs a PowerPoint to "get" you?

They're not ready for your kind of magic anyway.

Say what you do like, it's a spell.

Let them feel it before they understand it.

Let them *catch up.*

You're not hard to explain.

You're just not meant to be *contained.*

Chapter 7

Not Every Path Deserves a Destination

Let's rip off the band-aid right at the start:
Starting something and not finishing it doesn't make you flaky.

It makes you *self-aware*.
But try telling that to a world that's obsessed with stick-to-it-aliveness, commitment, and finishing everything you start like it's a moral obligation.
"Don't quit."
"See it through."
"Follow through, or you're not serious."
You know what's worse than quitting?
Staying stuck in something that no longer fits — just to prove you're not a quitter.

You're Not a Quitter. You're an Editor.

You're allowed to try something and realize it's not for you.
You're allowed to change your mind mid-way.
You're allowed to evolve *while* in motion.
That's not quitting.
That's **editing your life in real time.**
Think about it: writers cut entire chapters. Designers scrap entire versions. Musicians shelve albums that don't feel right.
They're not failures. They're professionals with taste.
So why do we shame ourselves when we outgrow a project, a path, or a plan?

Personal Story: The Thing I Didn't Finish (and Why That's Okay)

There was a time I launched something I thought I really wanted, a digital offer that blended career clarity, strategy, and a little soul.
It looked good on paper. It sounded great in DMs.
I had the checkout page, the content, and the marketing ready to go.
And two days in, I just... couldn't.
It wasn't resistance. It wasn't fear.
It was a *knowing.*
A full-body "This isn't it anymore."
Now, a past version of me would've pushed through. Finished it. Delivered it with gritted teeth and a smile.
But I didn't.

I paused. I let it go. I pivoted.

And you know what happened? Nothing burned down. No one hunted me for refunds. My credibility didn't vanish into the void.

Instead?

I felt relieved.

Once I took off the costume, I couldn't even recall that there was an itch in the first place.

The World Worships Finishers — Until They Burn Out

We applaud the person who finishes the marathon — even if they're limping across the line bleeding.

But what if the strongest move is stepping off the course before it breaks you?

The truth is: most of us were taught to value consistency over honesty.

To equate quitting with failure.

To see every pivot as a sign of weakness.

But you know what pivoting actually is?

It's data.

Your inner system is giving you feedback. And the people who *win* in life are the ones who listen early, not the ones who wait for the full crash.

Let's Redefine What "Sticking With It" Means

You're allowed to "stick with" things that are true to you, *not* things that are eating away at your soul.

Sticking with something just because you started it?

That's ego. That's performance. That's martyrdom dressed as

discipline.
Let it go.
Even if you told everyone about it.
Even if you spent money on it.
Even if you made a whole Canva carousel for it.
You get to change your mind.
No permission slip needed.

Let's Talk About Rihanna

Rihanna didn't release an album for years.
You know what she did instead?

- Built Fenty Beauty and disrupted the cosmetics industry
- Launched Savage X Fenty and redefined lingerie represen-
  tation
- Grew into a billionaire
- Had a baby and headlined the Super Bowl

She didn't "quit music." She *pivoted powerfully.*
And when she did come back to the stage, she did it on *her* terms
— as a full-spectrum woman, not just the version the world
wanted.
She didn't explain herself.
She *evolved out loud.*
Be like Rihanna. Quit. Pivot. Reclaim. Re-enter.
Whatever the season calls for.

Quitting Isn't a Failure, It's a Filter

When you quit something, you're not throwing your progress away.
You're keeping the insight. The skills. The lessons.
You're subtracting what no longer belongs.
It's not backtracking.
It's *course correction.*
And honestly? Some of your best pivots will come from things you were brave enough to walk away from.
You didn't fail.
You flourish.

When People Ask, "So What Happened With That Thing?"

People love consistency, not because they care about your growth, but because they love a tidy story.
So when you start and stop something, you'll get the classic:
"Whatever happened to that project you were working on?"
"Didn't you say you were launching that program?"
"I thought you were doing XYZ?"
Smile. Nod. And say:
"It served its purpose. Now I'm doing what actually aligns."
That's it.
You don't owe them a post-mortem.
You owe yourself *peace.*

For the Ones Who Are Hesitating Right Now

If you're sitting on something that you no longer feel connected
to, but you're scared of what people will think if you stop...
Here's your permission to close the tab.
Cancel the launch.
Change the major.
Archive the draft.
Pause the podcast.
Exit the collab.
Pull the plug.
Quit the job.
Not because it's not good.
But because it's not *you* anymore.
And that's the difference between consistency and clarity.

Your Identity Isn't Tied to a Project

Let me say this loud for the ones in the back:
You are not what you finish.
You are who you become through the process.
Starting something and stopping it doesn't make you inconsis-
tent.
It makes you *tuned in.*
Your ability to let go is a flex.
Your pivots are power moves.
Your false starts are compost for better ideas.

Really lean in to this

You don't need to see everything through to be valid.
You don't need a trophy at the end to call it meaningful.
You don't need to stay in the same direction just because you
were loud about it on social media.
You're allowed to be excited about something one month and
done with it the next.
That's not failure.
That's *clarity in motion*.
Let the world keep chasing finish lines.
You? You're here to follow the truth, your truth — wherever it
leads.
And sometimes, truth means knowing when to stop.
That's not quitting.
That's unboxing.

Chapter 8

ROI - Return on Imagination

Let's start with a sacred truth no one prints on productivity planners:

Your joy doesn't have to pay rent.

Seriously. Read it again.

You can paint without selling them.

You can sing without making an album.

You can create programs without turning them into a funnel.

You can sculpt clay without slapping a price tag on it.

Every passion you have doesn't have to scale, launch, go viral, get monetized, or become a damn side hustle.

Some things exist *only* to make you feel alive.

And that is reason enough.

Hustle Culture Wants Your Hobbies

We live in a world where the moment you're good at something...
.*bam*, here comes the unsolicited business advice.
"You should sell this."
"You could totally make a course out of that."
"Why don't you start a YouTube channel?"
"Omg you need to monetize this!"
No. No you don't.
Not everything has to become an offer.
Not every interest has to be optimised and shared with the world.
Because the second you turn every curiosity into a commercial offer, you stop being a human and start being a product.

I Almost Monetized the Joy Right Out of Myself

There was a time I was creating clay altarware purely because it grounded me.
No content calendar. No pricing model. Just clay, music, and magic.
And of course, people started asking,
"Are you selling these?"
"You should totally open a store!"
And I almost did. Because that's what we're taught to do, right?
But somewhere between SKU spreadsheets and packaging ideas, I felt it.
The joy was... fading.
That giddy feeling of making something just because my hands wanted to? Gone.

It was replaced with questions like, "Is this sellable?" "Would people buy this?" "Is this too niche?"

And I realized: **just because you *can* monetize something doesn't mean you *should*.**

So I took a breath. Put the business plans away.

And let my creativity be free again.

And suddenly? The joy came back.

Capitalism Will Try to Colonize Your Joy

Let's get blunt:

We all live in a system that doesn't know what to do with joy unless it can extract profit from it.

- You start dancing again? Time to become a dance reel influencer.
- You write for fun? Self-publish it and build a passive income funnel.
- Do you like healing? Start a spiritual coaching biz and hit 6 figures in six months.

NO.

Let your joy be sovereign.

Let your hobbies be useless in the best way.

Let your passions be *pleasure*, not pressure.

The moment you attach productivity to every passion, you lose the softness. The spark. The soul.

Signs You've Monetized Too Much

Here's a quick vibe check.
If you:

- Can't remember the last time you created something without sharing it
- Feel guilty doing things that don't "move the needle"
- Immediately ask "how can I monetise this?" after every new skill.
- Don't feel joy, just strategy.

Then, babe... hustle culture has entered the chat.
And it's time to exit the group.

You Are More Than Your Output

You're not a machine. You're a galaxy of urges, ideas, feelings, and flavor.
You get to bake just because.
You get to take dance classes with no plan to perform.
You get to sketch, sculpt, sing, design, grow herbs, embroider, act, journal, all without needing to explain it to anyone.
There is nothing wrong with wanting to build businesses.
But don't confuse purpose with productivity.
And don't confuse monetization with meaning.
Sometimes, what feeds your soul is the thing no one else even

sees.
And that's okay.

Say This With Me:

"Just because I'm good at something doesn't mean I owe it to the marketplace."
Read it. Tattoo it. Write it on your bathroom mirror.
Not every gift is meant to be sold.
Some are meant to be sacred.
The moment you feel the pressure to sell, your joy... pause.
Ask: *Would I still do this if no one paid me, praised me, or posted about it?*
If the answer is yes, protect it like your peace depends on it.
Because it probably does.

What If You Made Things Just for the Joy of It?

Imagine this:
You wake up and create something without thinking about ROI.
You make art without building a content calendar around it.
You read without turning it into a book club.
You dance without recording it.
You play just to play.
That's not laziness.
That's *life force* in motion.
Let your inner child run the show sometimes.

She's not here for the hustle.
She's here for wonder.

When People Ask, "Are You Going to Turn This Into Something?"

Here's your script:
"Nope. It's just for me."
Then sip your tea like royalty and move on.
You don't owe the world an explanation for your joy.
You don't have to justify rest, pleasure, or play.
You don't need a content strategy for your soul.

For the Ones Who Used to Love It

If you've fallen out of love with something you *used* to adore...
Maybe it's not that the passion died.
Maybe it got buried under strategy, structure, and sales funnels.
Try doing it again like no one's watching.
No monetisation plan.
No pressure to be good.
Just *you* and the thing that made your insides sparkle.
If you can find your way back to joy, even for five minutes, it's not gone.
You're just one "hell no" to hustle away from it.

Remember...

You are allowed to keep some things just for yourself.
Not everything you love has to be productive.
Not every curiosity needs a conversion rate.
Not every skill needs to be sold.
You're allowed to create without capitalism breathing down your neck.
Protect your joy like it's your last match in a world full of wet blankets.
Because in the end, it's not the things you sold that make you feel whole.
It's the things you loved enough *not* to.

Chapter 9

Career Paths Are for Robots. You're a Revolution

Build your own roadmap instead of choosing one path forever.
Let's get one thing straight: the traditional idea of a "career path" is outdated. It's stiff. It's dusty. And let's be honest, it was designed for factories, not for multi-passionate human beings like you.

You've been told to pick one lane.

Master one thing.

Stick to your industry.

And maybe, just maybe, after 30 years and a few promotions, you'll get a gold watch and a polite farewell email.

But what if you're someone who wants to write code and write poetry?

Launch a startup and launch a podcast?

Lead teams by day and work with energy by night?

You are not confused. You are not unfocused. You are *abundant*.

And it's time the world caught up with that.

The "Pick One Thing" Myth

You've heard it:

"Jack of all trades, master of none."

"Stay in your lane."

"You'll confuse people."

Spoiler alert: most people are already confused about their own lives, and that is not your problem.

What you *can* be is a master of integration. A master of stacking. A master of taking seemingly different pieces of yourself and building something bigger, smarter, and more soul-aligned than any single label career could offer.

Linear careers are a myth. Real ones look like constellations: messy, magical, and interconnected.

Real Talk: I Built My Own Map

I didn't wake up one day and say, "I want to do a dozen things at once." I followed the breadcrumbs. I started in tech. That's what paid the bills. But my soul was whispering something else. Teach. Heal. Create. Speak. Write. Lead.

At first, I tried to silence those whispers. I thought I had to choose. I thought being taken seriously meant "staying consistent."

But what's more powerful than consistency? *Wholeness.*

So I let myself become a Technology leader who reads Akashic Records. The engineering manager who crafts goddess altars out of clay. The strategist who guides breathwork rituals. I stopped contorting myself to fit into boxes I had long outgrown. And guess what? The more I owned all of me, the more magnetic my work became. Because people can *feel* when you're walking your full truth.

It's rare. It's radical. And it's irresistible.

Meet the Multi-Passion Moguls

You're not the only one rewriting the rules. Here are a few women who've made a career out of *being many things*, not in spite of it, but because of it.

Mindy Kaling : A Cultural Architect

She didn't just act, she wrote, produced, and reshaped representation in comedy. From *The Office* to *The Mindy Project* to *Never Have I Ever*, Mindy built her own universe, centring brown girls who are messy, funny, brilliant, and powerful. She didn't wait for permission, she created the roles she wasn't getting. That's called owning the narrative.

Masaba Gupta : A Rule-Breaker-in-Chief

Fashion designer. Actor. CEO. Masaba turned her love for bold patterns and storytelling into a fashion empire and then flipped the script by starring in a Netflix series about her own life. She runs multiple brands, appears on screen, and redefines what it means to be a modern Indian woman in business. Masaba isn't "doing too much." She's *doing it all* on her terms.

Neha Bagaria : A Biotech Entrepreneur. Tech Founder. Women's Advocate.

Neha went from building a biotech company to taking a break for motherhood — and came back with a vengeance to build *JobsForHer*, India's largest career platform for women returning to work. She fused purpose and platform, tech and social impact, business and boldness. Her career isn't a straight line — it's a power curve.

Build Your Multi-Passion Career Like a Pro

Let's get practical. Here's how to build your own multi-passionate roadmap, no fluff, no clichés.

1. Start With Your Soul Stack

Write down everything that lights you up. Not just what you're "good at," but what feels like *home*. What do people always ask you about? What could you lose hours doing?

Now group them. See what patterns emerge. Maybe your love for analysis and your obsession with human behavior = business coaching. Maybe design + ritual = spiritual branding.

Your genius lives in the overlap.

2. Design Offers, Not Titles

Forget trying to fit into someone else's job description. Design your own offers. Think:

- What do I want to *create* in the world?
- How do I want to help people?

- Can I teach, build, design, speak, coach, heal, or blend them?

Think like a studio, not a single service provider. You're not "just" anything.

3. Stack Your Experience, Don't Scrap It
You don't need to throw your old life away to build a new one. Use your past roles as ingredients in your next chapter.
You worked in QA? Cool—bring that precision into product design.
You were a teacher? Use that empathy in stakeholder workshops.
Everything counts. Everything stacks.

4. Rotate the Spotlight
Your passions don't all need to shine at the same time. Think of the seasons. Some years, you're writing. Some years, you're coaching. Some years, you're launching something wild no one saw coming.
It's not an inconsistency. It's *dynamic alignment.*

5. Define Success On Your Terms
You can't measure a multi-passionate career with someone else's ruler.
For you, success might look like:

- Doing meaningful work and taking creative risks
- Having space to rest and dream
- Being known for your essence, not just your title

So ask yourself regularly:

Am I fulfilled? Am I challenged? Am I *free*?
If yes, you're winning.

Your Career Is a Living Ecosystem

You are not a brand. You are not a product. You are not a five-year plan.
You are a whole damn ecosystem.
You have roots and wings. Cycles and shifts.
Some things bloom early. Some take time. Some need pruning.
But everything you've done? It belongs. It matters. It's part of the whole.
Let your career grow with you. Let it change. Let it make sense *after* you've lived it, not before.
You don't owe the world a consistent version of you.
You owe yourself the freedom to evolve, loudly and proudly.
Let people watch you pivot. Let them whisper. Let them misunderstand.
You're not here to fit in.
You're here to *show* what's possible when you stop asking permission and start owning your creative power.
Reminder :
You don't have to shrink your story to fit a title.
You don't have to pick one lane when your soul is building an entire city.
They told you to specialise.
You decided to *expand.*
Because your career isn't a path.
It's a playground.

A temple.
A revolution in motion.

Chapter 10

Make Your Brand Work With You, Not On You

Let's be honest.

The internet is overflowing with people who sound the same.

Every bio reads like a recycled LinkedIn headline. Every post starts with "I help..." or ends with "Let me know your thoughts!"

And somewhere in the middle, the real *you* gets lost.

It's not your fault. Most of us were taught that personal branding is about positioning, polish, and "professionalism."

But what if you could build a brand that feels like an *actual human being*?

One that reflects your weirdness, wisdom, warmth: not just your qualifications?

That's what this chapter is about.

Not building a brand that boxes you in.

But revealing one that frees you.

What Is a Brand, Really?

It's not your logo.
Not your Canva aesthetic.
Not that clever one-liner you keep tweaking in your bio.
Your brand is simply the **feeling** people get when they experience you online.
It's the tone of your writing. The stories you choose to share.
The way people feel after reading your post or watching your video.
If your content makes people say,
"Wait, who is this, and how do I work with them?", You've got a real brand.
If they scroll and forget you the minute they swipe away, you've got a resume in disguise.
Let's change that.

Part I: Why Most Brands Feel Flat (and What to Do About It)

You're not boring — so why does your content feel like beige wallpaper?
Here's why: most people show up online with a filter already on. Not the Instagram kind. The *emotional* kind.
The one that says:

- "Be professional."

- "Keep it safe."
- "Don't make it about you."
- "Stick to your niche."
- "Pick one thing."

So you water it down, round off the edges. Post what you *should* instead of what's actually real.
And what comes out is... bland. Safe. Predictable.
AKA: the cardboard version of yourself.

Try This: The Unfiltered Bio Check

Look at your bio. Your pinned post. Your about section.
Now ask yourself:
Would I say this to someone I like at a dinner table?
If not, rewrite it.
Here's how:

- Take the pressure off sounding like an "expert."
- Speak from a place of honesty and aligned energy.
- Add one line that would make your best friend laugh. Or nod. Or text you "omg so you."

That's when people start to recognize *you* and not just your profession.

Part II: Building a Brand That Feels Like Home

Now let's build a brand that works *for* you, not one you have to perform into every time you log on.

1. Speak in Your Real Voice

If you're witty IRL, be witty online. If you're blunt, be blunt. If you speak softly but with depth, let that show.
You don't need to "write like a creator."
You need to write like yourself.

Try This:
Take your last post or caption. Read it out loud.
Does it sound like a version of you that would make your actual friends roll their eyes?
If yes, rewrite it as a voice note. Start with "Hey, so here's what I've been thinking…"
Then do not overthink, just hit 'post'.

2. Post Before You're Ready

You don't have to wait until it's neat or fully processed.
Some of the most powerful content is messy, mid-thought, and deeply human.
Post it while it's still warm.
People resonate with real-time reflections more than perfectly packaged takeaways.
Mini Challenge:
Share something this week that you'd usually talk yourself out of.

Start the post with "I'm not sure how to say this, but…"
Let that be the permission slip.

3. Create from Your Lived Experience

You don't need to educate or prove your expertise constantly.
You can simply share what you *know* because you've lived it.
Instead of saying "5 tips for productivity," try:
"What I learned from crashing and burning trying to do everything at once."
or
"The one thing I changed that helped me stop hating Mondays."
This makes your brand feel lived in.
Not manufactured.

4. Blend, Don't Compartmentalize

Your brand doesn't have to be either spiritual or strategic.
Soft or sharp. Corporate or creative.
Let it be *both*. Let it be *you*.
Real-Life Example:
I've explained tech workflows using daily life examples.
I've brought breathwork into coaching calls.
I've used Akashic Records to reframe my business blocks.
That's not off-brand. That *is* the brand.
Because it's the truth of how I work.
Now it is your turn:

What's the one "unexpected" part of you that you haven't brought into your content yet?
Write one sentence that blends it in.

Example: "As someone who manages both Technical dashboards *and* moon rituals, here's what I've noticed..."

Part III: Making Your Brand Interactive

Here's the real secret to a brand that works for you:
It invites people in.
It doesn't just declare. It connects.

Add These Interactive Content Ideas and see how it works wonders

Fill-in-the-blank prompts:

- "If you knew me outside of work, you'd know I ___________."
- "Right now, I'm unlearning ___________ and learning ___________."
- "People think my work is about ___________, but it's really about ___________."

Polls & tiny asks:

- "Which version of my day do you want to hear about — the spreadsheet one or the spirit guide one?"
- "Do you feel more multi-passionate or niche-focused right now? Curious to know."

Human moments:

- Post a screenshot of your Notes app.

- Share a meme that made you laugh *too* hard.
- Write a caption like a text you'd send to a friend who "gets" your weirdness.

5. Let Your Visuals Match Your Voice

If you're bold but your brand colors look like sad oatmeal, let's change that.

You don't need a fancy shoot or designer (unless that excites you).

You just need congruence.

Your photos. Fonts. Filters. Even the way you write your captions, they should *feel* like you.

Quick Reframe:
Instead of "How do I look polished?"
Ask yourself: "How do I look *recognizable*?"

Part IV: Let Your Brand Work For You (Not the Other Way Around)

At the end of the day, your brand should feel like a home, not a trap.

You shouldn't need to put on a different version of yourself to hit publish.

You shouldn't have to shrink your story to fit a niche.

And you sure as hell don't need to become a marketing robot to be seen.

Your brand should make you feel more *yourself*, not less.

Let it be loud some days, soft others. Let it evolve. Let it pivot.
Let it carry all your contradictions with pride.
Because when your brand holds your *truth* —
you stop chasing clients and start attracting community.

Your Turn: The "This Is Me" Branding Jam

Use these fill-in-the-blank starters to shape your brand in your real voice.

1. I'm not for everyone, but I'm definitely for people who...

Example: ...get excited about both Airtable automations and moon cycles.

2. I don't just do ____________ — I also care deeply about ___________.

Example: I don't just do UX, I care deeply about how design makes people feel seen.

3. If you're into ____________ but hate ____________, you'll love hanging out here.

Example: If you're into soul work but hate spiritual bypassing, you'll love hanging out here.

Write three. Post one.
Let your people find you.
You don't need to go viral.
You don't need a niche that fits into a LinkedIn headline.
You don't need to be "the best" in your field.
You need to be *the best you.*

Because when your brand feels like a living extension of your soul, you don't burn out trying to "show up."
You just do.
And let people feel it.

Chapter 11

Stay Soft, Stay Steady, Stay You

Let's talk about the chaos.
The mental tabs that never close.
The idea list in your Notes app that's starting to look like a dissertation.
The energy spikes that push you into flow at 2 a.m., followed by the crash of decision fatigue by noon.
If you're multi-passionate, you know the drill.
Your brain isn't a straight line. It's a fireworks show.
Beautiful, brilliant, and sometimes... completely overwhelming.
So how do you *stay grounded* when your mind is always in motion?
Spoiler: it's not about shutting the tabs. It's about giving them a rhythm to dance to.

This chapter isn't about turning your brain off. It's about giving your brilliance a home base to return to. A system. A practice. A grounding cord that lets you fly without floating away.

The Myth of Consistency (for Brains Like Ours)

If you've ever felt guilty for not sticking to a schedule, welcome to the club.

We've been fed this narrative that success = routine, discipline, focus. That the only way to be taken seriously is to stick to one thing, one message, one timeline.

But multi-passionate brains aren't wired that way.

Your creativity doesn't run on Google Calendar.

It runs on *seasons* — energy surges, deep rest, and rapid bursts of clarity that don't always make logical sense.

You don't need a stricter system.

You need a rhythm that honors your natural flow.

My Story: The Year I Tried to Be "That Girl"

There was a year I decided to get "serious" about my life. I bought planners, color-coded schedules, and blocked out content calendars. I wanted to be *that girl* you know, the one who wakes up at 5 a.m., journals, green juices, batch creates a month of content, and glows from within.

It worked for three days. Maybe four.

But by day five, I was spiraling

Not because I lacked discipline, but because I was trying to force myself into a rhythm that didn't *belong* to me.

What saved me wasn't a productivity hack. It was a question

"What does grounding look like for *me*, not just aesthetically,

but energetically?"

That's when I stopped chasing routines and started building *rituals*.

Ritual vs. Routine: What's the Difference?

A **routine** is something you do because you feel like you should. A **ritual** is something you do because it brings you back to yourself.

Routines are rigid.

Rituals are rooted.

Routines get broken easily.

Rituals *hold you*, even when life gets chaotic.

As a multi-passionate creator, I needed rituals that gave me *just enough* structure without boxing me in.

Here are some that changed the game for me.

Ritual #1: The "No-Pressure Morning Drop-In"

Forget the 10-step morning routine. Most days, I just need 5 quiet minutes to ask myself:

What's the energy today?

What feels heavy?

What's calling me today?

Sometimes I write the answers.
Sometimes I just sit with them while sipping chai.
Sometimes I pull an oracle card, and on other days, I journal one messy sentence and move on.
It's not about discipline. It's about **checking in with myself before the world checks in on me**.
Try This:

Set a 5-minute timer. Ask yourself:
"What do I *need* today, and how do I feel about it?"

Ritual #2: "One Home Base Task Per Day"

With multiple ideas, projects, and roles, I used to try to tackle *everything* every day. That always ended in burnout and shame. Now, I anchor into one "home base" per day — the one thing I *commit* to finishing, no matter how scattered I feel.
Examples:

Monday = content writing

Tuesday = client sessions

Wednesday = admin

Thursday = creative play

Friday = flex / freeform

Everything else is a bonus. That's it.
Try This:
Assign one focus *theme* per day. Let that be your grounding anchor.

Ritual #3: "Brain-Dump to Breath" Ritual

My brain loves to buzz at night. Ideas, regrets, reminders, to-dos. All of it.
So now I use a simple ritual to clear it out:

Grab a notebook and dump everything in your mind. No filter.

Draw a line underneath it.

Then write:

1. What's mine to carry tomorrow?
2. What can wait?
3. What can I trust the universe to handle?

Then I do 3 rounds of deep belly breaths. Just to close the loop.
This isn't productivity. It's energetic hygiene.

Try This:

Before bed, try writing down all your open loops — then breathe like you're sealing an envelope. Done. Closed. Safe.

The Power of Anchoring Statements

Sometimes, grounding isn't about doing anything.
It's about **reminding yourself who you are** when your brain feels loud.
Here are a few of my anchoring statements. You're welcome to borrow them — or write your own:

"I don't have to do it all today."

"My pace is not a problem."

"I am allowed to love many things."

"Not every thought needs a plan."

"I can hold ideas without acting on them right now."

Post them on your mirror.
Make them your phone wallpaper.
Tattoo them on your soul.

Grounding Through the Body (Not Just the Mind)

Your mind might always be moving, but your body is your anchor.
When you're in a spiral of "too many tabs open," try dropping into your body with something *simple*:

A 30-second body shake

A walk without your phone

Tapping your chest and saying, "I'm right here."

Putting your hand on your belly and taking 3 deep breaths

It's not about being zen. It's about *returning*.

Try This:

Set a 2x daily "return to body" reminder. Even 1 minute counts.

Let's Talk About Guilt (Because It Shows Up a Lot)

Guilt is the default emotion of a multi-passionate mind.
You feel guilty for switching focus.
Guilty for forgetting an idea.
Guilty for not being consistent.
Guilty for wanting to do *everything*.
Here's what I need you to hear:
Your range is not a flaw. It's your rhythm.
You are not failing because your interests keep shifting.
You are evolving. Rapidly. Deeply. Unapologetically.
The more you build structures that *move with you*, the less you'll
feel like you're falling behind.

The "Now, Next, Later" Tracker

This simple tool changed my relationship with productivity. It gives my ideas a *place to land*, so I don't feel like I'm dropping balls.
Create three columns:

Now: What I'm actively working on

Next: What's coming up soon

Later: What I've parked for some other day

I personally use this in Notion, but you can write it in a notebook too.

Try This:
List your current projects under these 3 headers. Let "Later" hold the pressure for you.

Real-Life Story: The Week I Tried to Do Everything

There was a week when I genuinely thought I could juggle it all. I had a corporate deadline, a Reiki session to prep for, Instagram content to create, a podcast idea brewing, and for some reason, I had also decided to start a new digital product because "I was feeling inspired."
On paper, I had energy. In my head, I was hyped.
By day three, I was spiralling.

Not because I lacked capability, but because I had zero container for that capability.
I was chasing every idea without anchoring *any* of them.
What did I do?
Nothing fancy. I paused. I grabbed a sticky note. I wrote:

What's most alive right now?

What's draining me that I'm pretending isn't?

What can wait till next week?

Just that act of naming my energy and not judging it, not fixing it, brought me back to myself.
I didn't finish everything that week. But I finished the *right* things. The ones that felt rooted in my values.
And more importantly, I ended the week feeling like a human and not a content machine.

You Don't Need a System. You Need Soil.

Systems are helpful — but only when they grow from your truth.
You don't need to force your multi-passionate mind into neat little containers.
You just need **soil** — a few steady rhythms that keep you rooted while you reach in all directions.
This chapter isn't about mastering structure. It's about finding *rituals that feel like home.*
Let your rhythm be soft. Let it change. Let it be yours.

Your Grounding Toolkit:

Here's your grounding toolkit, recapped:

Morning Drop-In
Check in with your energy, not your to-do list.

One Focus Per Day
Anchor into one thing. Let the rest flow.

Brain-Dump + Breath Ritual
Clear the tabs. Seal the thoughts. Rest.

Anchoring Statements
Remind yourself who you are when your mind forgets.

Return to the Body
Move. Breathe. Tap in. You're here.

Now, Next, Later Tracker
Park the ideas. Prioritize peace.

Ritual Over Routine
Let your practices hold you, not control you.

You are not scattered. You are a symphony.
And your rhythm doesn't have to make sense to the world to be *sacred* to you.

Let it move.
Let it root.

Let it rise.

You're not too much.

You're just in motion.

And now... You know how to stay grounded and anchor into it.

Chapter 12

Stop Making Sense. Start Making Impact.

Let's begin with a feeling you probably know too well.
That moment when you're talking about all the things you love, and the person across from you tilts their head, squints slightly, and says:
"Wait, so... what do you actually *do?*"
It's not curiosity. It's confusion.
And the unspoken message underneath it is: *"Can you please simplify yourself to be more digestible?"*
Here's what I want you to remember in that moment:
You are not confusing or confused . You are layered. And the right people will feel the difference.

The Problem Was Never You. It Was the Box.

From childhood, we're trained to be clear and easy to understand.
"What do you want to be when you grow up?"
As if we're supposed to pick one answer and stay loyal to it forever.
We internalise this early. That a "clear" identity is a *narrow* one. That we need to make sense at dinner tables, on LinkedIn, or in our elevator pitch.
But here's the truth: when you're a multi-passionate human, you were *never meant* to make sense to people who've been taught to only see in straight lines.
And your job is not to contort your identity into something they can comprehend.
Your job is to *own the fullness* of who you are, even if it doesn't look like a single, simple sentence.

My Moment of Split

For years, I lived two lives.
In the day: a tech professional, team lead, process queen. In the background: a Reiki healer, Akashic reader, creative soul trying to breathe under all the productivity metrics.
I had two Instagram pages. Two voices. Two lives.
Every time I showed up online, I had to choose which self was "appropriate" to speak through.
I wasn't confused, I was split.
And let me tell you, being split is far more exhausting than being

seen as "too much."
Nothing wrong if you want to maintain two different pages, but you as a human being should be able to talk about it like, This is me, and This is also me!

The Day I Cracked the Code (Accidentally)

One day, I was on a client strategy call when I casually said, "Honestly, this whole project feels like a chakra blockage."
Dead silence.
I braced myself for the awkwardness.
Then one of the team leads said:
"Wait, that actually makes so much sense. Keep going."
That moment cracked something open. I realised I didn't have to choose between being strategic *or* spiritual. I could be both and in the same sentence, in the same body, in the same space. And the right people? They didn't get confused.
They felt *relieved*. Seen. Safe to bring their whole selves, too.

Why You Feel Misunderstood (And Why It's Not Your Fault)

Here's the thing: most people *don't* know how to engage with someone who operates outside the lines.
You talk about designing workflows and pulling Oracle cards.
You talk about your love for UX *and* mythology.
You teach business strategy but also burn incense and set intentions.

To a single-lane mind, that sounds like "a lot."
But to your people, the ones who also live in the intersections, it sounds like home.

Confusion Isn't About You. It's About Their Lens.

People aren't confused because you do many things.
They're confused because you haven't shown them the *thread* that ties it all together yet.
So stop trying to shrink yourself. Start highlighting your through-line.

Try This: Find Your Core Message

Ask yourself:

1. What do I help people feel or become, *no matter* what format I work in?
2. What truth keeps showing up across everything I do?
3. What's the one thing people thank me for, regardless of the service?

When you know what *you're really about*, you can stop explaining your job titles and start expressing your *essence*.

You Don't Have to Choose Simplicity Over Wholeness

People will say:

"But isn't it confusing if you talk about tech and spirituality?"

"Shouldn't you focus on just one thing?"

"Won't the clients get mixed messages?"

Here's the answer:
Only the *wrong* clients will.
The right ones will say:
"Oh my god, I didn't know I was allowed to be this whole."

Let's Talk About Branding (Without the Boring Part)

A lot of branding advice is built around the idea of *making it easier for others to define you.*
But here's a reframe:
Your brand shouldn't simplify you; it should *amplify your truth.*
You don't need a polished persona. You need coherence.
And coherence doesn't mean being "one thing."
It means every part of you is anchored in the *same frequency.*

Example: What Coherence Sounds Like

"I guide creative professionals through soul-aligned structure , whether I'm teaching them how to manage projects, host rituals, or redesign their brand."
That's not a list of titles. That's the truth. That's a lens.
When your message is rooted, your multi-dimensionality becomes a *feature*, not a bug.

What If They Still Don't Get It?

Let them go.
Seriously. Let them go.
Stop trying to prove yourself to people who need you to shrink before they'll respect you.
Those are not your people.
They never were.
Let your range filter the room for you.

Real Story: The Job Interview I Thought I Bombed (And Didn't)

A few years ago, I took on a leadership role in tech. During the interview, they asked me a question, How do you handle pressure?
Then I took a risk and I talked about energy work. Not because it was strategic, but because it was *true*.
I told them that I bring a deep emotional presence to technical spaces. That I care about both system logic and human energy.
One of the panellists furrowed her brow. The other smiled.
I left thinking I had overstepped.
Two days later, they made me an offer.
Why? Because I said the thing no one else did, the *right* person in the room felt it.

What's the Vibe People Feel When You Enter a Room?

Forget what you do for a second.
Ask yourself:

What's the energetic signature I leave behind?

Do people feel braver after talking to you?

Do they feel more creative? More grounded? More honest?

That's your brand.
Not your tagline. Not your aesthetic.

That *energy* is what creates recognition.

What's in Your Blend?

You don't need to "niche down." You need to *name your blend*.
What are your ingredients?
Mine is:

Emotional intelligence

Soul strategy

Tech intuition

Sacred storytelling

Now let's try yours.

What are the top four energies, themes, or languages you move in?
Write them down.
That's your signature blend.

You Are Not a Puzzle to Solve. You Are a Language to Learn.

And the people who are meant to learn it? They *will*.
They'll lean in. Ask questions. Stay curious.
They'll say:
"I don't fully get it... But I know it matters."
That's when you know they're ready for your range.

What to Remember When You Feel "Hard to Explain"

You are not confusing. You are layered.

You don't need to choose one thing — you need to find your thread.

The right people won't need you to shrink.

Your voice isn't too much. It's magnetic.

Coherence > Consistency. Let your energy match across formats.

People buy the clarity of truth, not the clarity of title.

Anchor Practice: One-Liner Rewrite

When you want to talk about yourself, not from your split self but from your whole self, I have you covered.

Let's rewrite your "what do you do?" answer from a lens of essence.

Formula:

I help/support/guide [who] through [blend of gifts] so they can [core transformation].

Example:

I help multi-passionate women lead their tech careers and soul paths with equal power through structure, strategy, and self-trust.

Now you try:

   → I help/support _______________________________________

____

   → using _______________________________________

____

   → so they can _______________________________________

____

Stick that on your About page. Your Instagram bio. Your mirror. Your heart.

You're Not the Problem. You're the Portal.

You're not too much. You're just the embodiment of a world they haven't learned to see yet.
You're the bridge between systems and soul.
Between logic and love.
Between excellence and emotion.
And when you own all of it, you stop looking for people to "get" you.
You start looking for people who *recognise* you.

The right people won't be confused by you.

They'll feel like they've finally found someone speaking their language.
And the rest?
Let them go.

Chapter 13

Presence Over Performance: Redefining Consistency for Real Humans

Let's just name the fear.

You want to be consistent.

You also want to stay *interesting*.

And somewhere along the way, you've equated "consistency" with being repetitive, mechanical, or watered down.

I get it.

The advice is everywhere:

"Post three times a week."

"Stick to your pillars."

"Be known for one thing."

But if you're multi-passionate, that kind of advice can feel like a death by content schedule.

So what do you do when your brain is a firework, your passions keep evolving, and the idea of posting the same tip in five different formats makes you want to run?

You rewrite what consistency means — *on your terms.*

What Consistency Isn't

Let's start by breaking the myths:

- It's not posting every day at 9 AM.
- It's not repeating the same message until you lose your personality.
- It's definitely not diluting your creativity just to be seen.

Consistency isn't sameness.
It's *recognition* at a soul level.
It's when people encounter your work and immediately feel, "This feels like them."
Even if the topic changes. Even if the format shifts.

You Don't Need to Be Predictable. You Need to Be Rooted.

Predictability is boring.
Rootedness is magnetic.
You can talk about twenty different things as long as they're all orbiting the *same sun*.
That sun could be your core values, your creative lens, your energetic vibe, or your personal story.
Whatever it is, *own it*. Then build your expressions around it.
People don't get tired of your message.
They get tired when you stop being *present* in your message.

My Truth: I Tried the Perfect Content Calendar and I burned out

There was a phase where I followed all the "content consistency" rules.
rules.
Monday: motivational quote.
Tuesday: carousel with 3 tips.
Wednesday: personal story.
Thursday: video.
Friday: sell.
Sounds good on paper.
But within two weeks, I felt like I was ghostwriting for a version of me I didn't even like.
The voice was mine, but the energy was missing.
What I needed wasn't a template. I needed *permission* to be present, to pivot, to play, and to be still consistent.
So I built something that honoured how I actually work.

Let's Reframe Consistency: Show Up, Don't Shrink

Here's the core idea:

Consistency is not about repeating content.
It's about being *recognisable* wherever you show up.

That means:

- You can shift topics — if your tone is anchored.
- You can try new platforms — if your energy is intact.
- You can take breaks, if your return is rooted in honesty.

Try This: Define Your "Consistency Anchors"

Instead of forcing yourself into a rigid calendar, build a rhythm around these three anchors:

1. Consistent Voice:
What's your truth-telling tone?
Are you the big sister?
The inner child?
The disruptor?
The space-holder?

2. Consistent Energy:
Do people come to you for clarity? Depth? Fire? Stillness? Insight? Humor?

3. Consistent Experience:
What's the vibe across your spaces? Can people trust that your brand *feels* the same on your feed, in your emails, and on a live call?
Lock those in, and your content can evolve all it wants.

Mini Exercise: Your Consistency Map

Fill in these blanks:

- "When people read my work, I want them to feel ______________."
- "My voice is a mix of ______________ and ______________."
- "Even if I talk about different things, my content always reflects ______________."

Use these answers as your compass, not your cage.

But What If I Get Bored?

Here's the truth: *You will.*
You're multi-passionate. You thrive on change, evolution, and experimentation.
So instead of avoiding boredom, let's *design for it.*
Ways to Stay Fresh Without Losing Consistency:

- Rotate themes each month. Let your curiosity lead your content.
- Build series instead of one-offs. "5 Days of Me," "Sunday Stories," "Unfiltered Tuesdays."
- Reuse old content, but remix it to fit where you are now.
- Speak to the same truth through different lenses: story, metaphor, tip, question, and visual.
- Let your followers vote on topics. Give them the mic.

Remember: consistency doesn't mean you're a content machine.

It means you're a *living rhythm.*

Real Story: When I Took a Break (And Came Back Louder)

A while ago, I went silent online for weeks. Not because I had nothing to say, but because I had *too much*, and none of it felt ready.
When I came back, I didn't apologise. I just started where I was.
I wrote:
"I didn't ghost you. I was just talking to my soul for a while."
And that post got more resonance than anything I'd written in months.
Here's the lesson: *Presence beats frequency every time.*
Your people don't need you to be perfect.
They need you to be *in it.*
Real, evolving, and reachable.

The Power of Rhythmic Visibility

Instead of thinking in terms of "posting schedules," think in terms of *rhythmic visibility.*
That means:

- You don't ghost for 3 months and then dump 27 posts in a week.
- You create touchpoints that feel natural to you.
- You show up at a pace that's sustainable — emotionally,

energetically, and creatively.

Your rhythm could be:

- Weekly voice memo posts
- Bi-weekly deep dive blogs
- Daily stories with spontaneous thoughts
- Monthly newsletters that wrap up your inner world

Find what feels good. Stick with it until it doesn't. Adjust accordingly. That *is* consistency.

Notes for the Overthinker in You

You might be wondering:

- "Will people forget me if I'm not consistent?"
- No. People remember resonance more than routine.
- "What if I lose momentum?"
- You're not a brand. You're a human. You don't owe the algorithm your soul.
- "What if I don't feel inspired?"
- Then don't force it. But stay connected. Let people in on your pause, not just your polished version.

What Real Consistency Looks Like

Let's make this simple:

- You're consistent when your voice feels familiar
- You're consistent when your energy stays honest
- You're consistent when your message evolves with you
- You're consistent when you create from connection, not pressure

Your job isn't to be the loudest.
It's to be the most *you*, as often as your heart can sustain.
You don't have to be predictable to be professional.
You don't have to post daily to be impactful.
You just have to show up with clarity, honesty, and soul.
The right people will stay.

Unboxable Presence + Visibility Planner

For showing up in the world without losing yourself in the process

Why This Exists

You don't have to be everywhere, for everyone, all the time.
This isn't about being hyper-visible.
It's about staying *connected* to your truth, your energy, and your impact.

This is for when you want to stay in motion without spinning out.

To be present in your work, relationships, art, or leadership, without burning out.

Let's plan for that.

Step 1: What Does "Being Visible" Mean to Me Right Now?

Visibility is personal. For you, it might mean:

- Speaking up in a meeting
- Taking up space at the dinner table
- Launching a project
- Leading a conversation
- Showing your face again after a hard season
- Simply getting out of your head and into your day

Right now, visibility looks like:

→ ____

_______________   _______________

→ ____

____

Step 2: Define Your Presence Energies

What do you want people to feel when they're in your presence whether online, or in person, or energetically?

Choose 3 words that anchor how you want to show up:

Energy 1: ___________________

Energy 2: _______________

Energy 3: _______________

Examples: grounded, clear, open, brave, calm, playful, intentional, magnetic

Step 3: Map Your Rhythms

Instead of rigid schedules, we use *rhythmic touchpoints* — soft anchors that keep you grounded in presence.

Day	Energy Level	Presence Practice	Notes
Monday	Low	10 min grounding walk	
Tuesday	Medium	Reach out to one person	
Wednesday	High	Lead, teach, speak, create	
Thursday	Inspired	Journal or create space to rest	
Friday	Open	Check in: What needs my attention?	

Now build your own:

Day	Energy Level	Presence Practice	Notes

Step 4: Practice Showing Up Gently

Choose 3 small, soul-aligned ways you can stay present with yourself and others this week:

1.
2.
3.
4.
5.
6.

Examples: Answer one message with full attention. Wear something that makes you feel like yourself. Say "no" without over-explaining.

Step 5: Recommit Without Rigidity

What will I do if I miss a day?

→ ____

____

→ ____

____

What reminder do I want to come back to when I feel scattered?

→ ____

____

Presence Over Performance

You don't have to do it all. You don't have to do it perfectly. You just have to return, again and again to the version of you that's rooted, honest, and ready to be seen in whatever way feels right for *this* season.

That's what real visibility looks like.

Chapter 14

Forget the Title. Tell the Story.

Let's get one thing straight.
Your career is not a ladder. It's not a checklist. And it's definitely not a neatly organised series of promotions.
Your career is a *story*.
A living, breathing journey.
Full of pivots, pauses, left turns, rebirths, wild experiments, and moments that don't always make sense on paper, but make *you* who you are.
And that's not a weakness.
That's the point.

Where the Old Narrative Fails Us

We were taught to value linearity.
Study hard → Get the degree → Land the job → Climb the ladder → Retire with a legacy.
But what if you changed industries?
What if you took a break for your health, or your child, or your

art?
What if you spent five years learning an entirely new skill that lit you up more than your old title ever did?
Does that make your career "confusing"?
No. It makes it *alive*.

Why Your Story > Your Title

You know what people actually remember?
Not your certifications. Not your exact job role.
They remember the moment you told them how you navigated a career break with grace.
They remember how you talked about building your creative practice while working in IT.
They remember the light in your eyes when you shared what you're building now, even if it's different from what you built before.
Your job title may change a dozen times.
Your story — when told with honesty and courage — becomes your constant.

Real Talk: I've Been Many Things

I've been the BA, the product manager, the spiritual guide, the content strategist, the mentor, the artist.
At first, I thought I had to choose.
Then I realised I didn't. I just had to *own* the journey.

Each season added something.

Tech taught me structure. Healing taught me presence. Teaching taught me how to hold space.

Put them together? That's a skill stack. A story. A signature no one else can copy.

The zigzag isn't a detour. Its design.

What Hiring Managers (and Humans) Actually Want

Despite what some rigid recruiters might say, the best leaders and collaborators don't care about your tidy titles. They care about:

- Can you adapt?
- Can you tell a story that makes people care?
- Can you connect the dots between your past and what you're offering now?

That's not called being "scattered."
That's called having *range*.
If your LinkedIn looks non-linear, that's not a red flag. That's a conversation starter.

Story Break: Meet Poorvi

Poorvi started in architecture. She loved design but hated office politics. She pivoted into freelance interior work, then unexpectedly got into course design and educational tech.
When we first talked, she said, "I'm all over the place. No one will take me seriously."
I asked her one question: "What's the most common thing you care about in both roles?"
After a pause, she said, "I think I've always cared about *how people experience space.*
Whether that's a physical room or an online course."
Boom. That's her story.
She didn't need to erase her past. She needed to narrate it.

Reframe: From Job History to Signature Journey

Next time you're crafting your CV, LinkedIn profile, or elevator pitch, don't list titles. Tell a mini-arc.
Start here:

1. What pulled you into your first "real" role?
2. When did something shift in you, and how did you respond?
3. What values stayed constant, even when your jobs changed?
4. What are you building *now* that ties it all together?

You don't need to prove your "loyalty" to a job title.
You need to show *ownership* of your evolution.

What to Say When People Ask "So What Do You Do?"

That question isn't just about work. It's about *identity*. And it can trigger all the inner voices that say you're doing it wrong.
Here's your permission slip:
You don't owe anyone a polished, final-sounding answer.
Try saying:

- "Right now, I'm exploring…"
- "I work at the intersection of…"
- "I help people through a mix of…"
- "I've done a few things, but the thread through all of it is…"

Keep it real. Keep it alive. Let it change.
Because your answer can evolve — and still be valid.

When You Start Feeling Behind…

If you've ever thought,
"I'm not where I should be by now,"
Just know this
There is no single timeline.
No finish line, you're late for.
Every season you've lived through — even the quiet ones, even the messy ones — gave you something.
A skill. A scar. A story.
You don't need to "catch up."

You need to connect the dots from *here*.

Try This: Your Story Threads Map

Draw a simple 3-column grid.

Past Roles or Projects	What You Learned or Loved	What That Shows About You

Now read it back. You'll start to see your story emerging.
Not in job titles.
In threads of truth.

You Are the Through-Line

You don't need your career to be linear.
You need to remember that *you* are the consistent force within it.
The ideas you return to.
The values you show up with.

The way you make people feel.

Those are your anchor points.

Those are your brand.

Those are your power.

Your career path doesn't have to make sense to a stranger at a networking event.

It only has to feel aligned to the version of *you* that's here now — and the version of you you're becoming next.

Because the title may change.

The story might evolve.

But your power?

That's already here.It's in the truth of your journey, not the straightness of it.

Chapter 15

You're Not a Persona. You're a Presence.

Let's end where most of us begin, with the fear that we are *too much*.
Too loud.
Too sensitive.
Too smart.
Too weird.
Too spiritual.
Too logical.
Too ambitious.
Too emotional.
Too many interests.
Too many pivots.
Too many contradictions.
Too. Damn. Much.
We try to shrink ourselves to fit. Round out the edges. Speak a little softer. Stay in one lane. Do not make waves.
And in doing so, we lose touch with the most important truth of all:

You're not too much.
You're everything you were always meant to be.

Let's Get Honest: You Were Never Meant to Be One Thing

There's a reason this book is called *Unboxable.*
Because some of us were born to be *too expansive* to fit a single title, a narrow lane, a 3-line bio.
Your range? It isn't a liability.
Your depth? It isn't a phase.
Your curiosity, your intensity, your duality — all of it is *by design.*
You don't need to tone it down.
You need to *build a life big enough* to hold it.

You've Always Known

Even when you tried to follow the rules.
Even when you chase "clarity."
Even when you stayed small to stay safe.
You knew.
There was more.
More of you. More to say. More to create. More ways to be.
Not more for the sake of hustle, but more because you are *not* one-dimensional.
You're a galaxy. A system. A full-spectrum soul.

This Isn't About Doing It All. It's About Being All of You

Being *everything you need to be* doesn't mean you'll be productive 24/7 or master 19 careers at once.

It means you stop hiding the parts of yourself that don't "fit the narrative."

It means you stop apologising for wanting more than most people understand.

It means you stop asking for permission to be who you *already are.*

Real Talk: You Can Stop Performing Now

You don't need to play the role anymore.

The "put-together professional."

The "sweet spiritual one."

The "always-in-control leader."

The "niche content creator."

The "normal" version of yourself that doesn't make others uncomfortable.

You don't need to shrink to belong.

You don't need to edit yourself into palatable pieces.

You are not a persona. You are a *presence.*

A Message for When You Start to Shrink Again

Because you will, we all do.
In rooms where you're the only one like you.
When you're misunderstood.
When someone makes you feel like you're "too much" again.
Here's what I want you to remember in those moments:
"Their confusion is not my cue to shrink.
My job is not to be easier to digest.
My job is to be real and keep growing."
Say it out loud if you need to.
Tattoo it on your heart if you must.

A Reminder: You Built This

You read this book.
You let yourself be seen.
You reclaimed your voice, your rhythm, your story, your contradictions.
You said yes to your whole self.
You did this.
Not a mentor. Not a brand coach. Not a perfect plan.
You.
So trust that if you could come this far, you can build the rest too.
Build the offers. The rituals. The career. The art. The relationships. The systems.
Build it in your voice. In your way. In your season.

Let Them Watch You Expand

There will always be people who don't get it.
Let them be confused.
There will always be people who want you to stay small.
Let them want.
There will always be voices (internal and external) that say, "pick one thing."
Let them echo.
And then keep growing anyway.
Because every time you take up space, as all of you, you give someone else the courage to do the same.

Final Journal Prompts (for the road ahead)

1. **What part of me am I no longer willing to hide to make others comfortable?**

   → ______________________________________

   ____

2. **If I stopped asking "how do I make this clear?" and started asking "how do I make this *true*?" — what would shift?**

   → ______________________________________

   ____

3. **What would it look like to build a life that's not just impressive, but deeply *me*?**

   → ______________________________________

And Finally: A Blessing for the Unboxable Ones

May you stop seeking validation from small rooms.

May you find people who mirror your magic, not question it.

May your art be wild. Your career is yours. Your voice be unfiltered.

Remember: your range is not your weakness. It's your revolution.

You're not too much.

You're a whole damn universe.

And you are finally coming home.

www.ingramcontent.com/pod-product-compliance
Lightning Source LLC
Chambersburg PA
CBHW040805120726
48005CB00012B/1308